D1256061

Crayola World of PURPLE

Mari Schuh

Lerner Publications ◆ Minneapolis

For the wonderful first-grade students at St. John Vianney School

Official Licensed Product
Lerner Publications Company
A division of Lerner Publishing Group, Inc.
241 First Avenue North
Minneapolis, MN 55401 USA

For reading levels and more information, look up this title at www.lernerbooks.com.

Main body text set in Mikado a Medium 20/28.
Typeface provided by HVD Fonts.

Library of Congress Cataloging-in-Publication Data

Names: Schuh, Mari C., 1975- author. | Crayola (Firm)
Title: Crayola world of purple / by Mari Schuh.
Other titles: World of purple
Description: Minneapolis : Lerner Publications, [2020] | Series: Crayola world of color | Audience: Ages 5–9. | Audience: K to grade 3. | Includes bibliographical references and index.
Identifiers: LCCN 2018038341 (print) | LCCN 2018039299 (ebook) | ISBN 9781541561397 (eb pdf) | ISBN 9781541554696 (lb : alk. paper)
Subjects: LCSH: Purple–Juvenile literature. | Color in nature–Juvenile literature. | Colors–Juvenile literature. | Crayons–Juvenile literature.
Classification: LCC QC495.5 (ebook) | LCC QC495.5 .S3687227 2020 (print) | DDC 535.6–dc23

LC record available at https://lccn.loc.gov/2018038341

Manufactured in the United States of America
1-45787-42669-11/21/2018

CONTENTS

Hello, Purple!

Where can you find **purple** in your world?

Purple is all around us.
Look for **violet**, **royal purple**,
and **plum**.

Purple in Nature

Colorful lilacs and crocuses open their petals. Spring will be here soon!

See **purple** fill the night sky.

A thunderstorm is near!

Purple covers the land. Tulips grow as far as the eye can see.

Purple **Animals**

Purple lives high in the trees. See a violet-backed starling or a lesser **purple** emperor butterfly flit its wings!

13

Purple swims in oceans and aquariums. Sea stars float near coral reefs.

Purple **Foods**

Purple grows all summer long. Water and sunlight help eggplants and onions grow big and round.

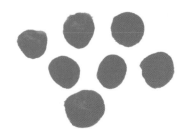

You can find **purple** growing on the vine.

Eat grapes one by one!

Purple **Where You Live**

Purple zooms down the highway. Trucks carry goods to faraway places. What might be inside?

Bundle up!

Purple is cozy. Crochet purple yarn into warm scarves and blankets.

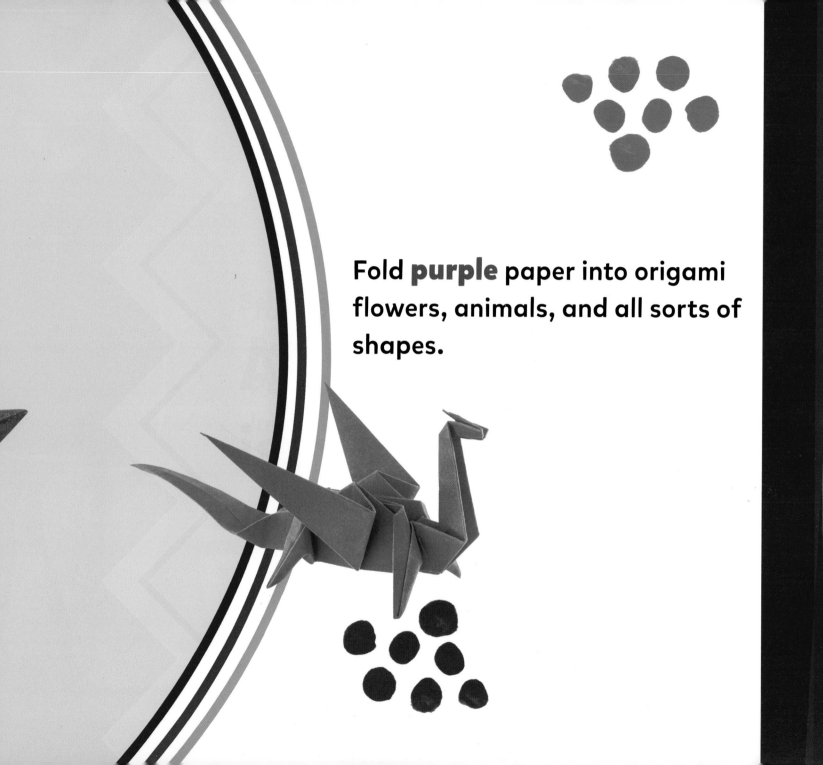

Fold **purple** paper into origami flowers, animals, and all sorts of shapes.

A soccer team is ready to play.
Go, **purple**!

Where will you see **purple** next?

Color with Purple!

Purple is fun! Draw a picture with only **purple** crayons.
Which shades will you choose to use?

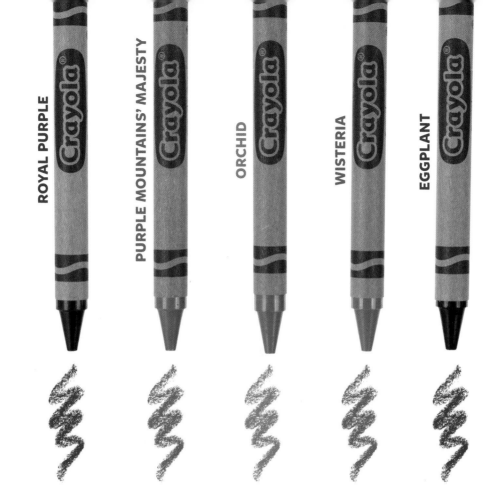

ROYAL PURPLE

PURPLE MOUNTAINS' MAJESTY

ORCHID

WISTERIA

EGGPLANT

Purple All around You

If we look around, we can find **purple** almost anywhere. Here are some Crayola® crayon shades of **purple** used in this book. Which shade do you like best?

Glossary

aquarium: a glass tank where people can see fish and other ocean life

crochet: needlework done by weaving loops in a thread with a hooked needle

good: an item for sale

origami: the art of folding paper

reef: an area of sand, rock, or coral that is close to the ocean's surface

shade: a color's lightness or darkness

thunderstorm: a rainstorm that has thunder and lightning

vine: a plant with a long, thin stem that grows along the ground or climbs on fences and trees

To Learn More

Books

Cantillo, Oscar. *Purple around Me*. New York: Cavendish Square, 2015.
Read about where else you can find this bright color.

Shepherd, Jodie. *Crayola Spring Colors*. Minneapolis: Lerner Publications, 2018.
Purple is one of many colors we see in spring. Read this book to learn about all the pretty spring colors.

Websites

Purple Coloring Page
http://www.kidzone.ws/prek_wrksht/colors/colors-purple1.htm
Have fun coloring things that are purple!

Unicorn in Space
http://www.crayola.com/free-coloring-pages/print/unicorn-in-space-coloring-page/
Use purple crayons to color a fun space scene.

Index

Photo Acknowledgments

Image credits: Corbis royalty free, p. 2; Martin Valigursky/Shutterstock.com, p. 4 (city); Albert Russ/Shutterstock.com, p. 4 (gem); Donald Miralle/Getty Images, p. 5 (football players); humbak/Shutterstock.com, pp. 5, 15 (starfish); Fesus Robert/Shutterstock.com, p. 5 (lavender field); Ilona Nagy/Moments/Getty Images, p. 6; irina02/Shutterstock.com, pp. 6-7; George Lepp/Photographer's Choice/Getty Images, pp. 8-9; Ganeshkumar Dura/Shutterstock.com, pp. 10-11; Gail Shumway/Photographer's Choice RF/Getty Images, p. 12; Dave Montreuil/Shutterstock.com, pp. 12-13; Preediwat/Shutterstock.com, pp. 14-15; Siriwan_B/Shutterstock.com, p. 16; nuttakit/iStock/Getty Images, pp. 16-17; oersin/iStock/Getty Images, pp. 18-19; Martin Charles Hatch/Shutterstock.com, p. 20; Jacek_Sopotnicki/iStock/Getty Images, pp. 20-21; JenDen2005/iStock/Getty Images, pp. 22-23; i9370/iStockGetty Images, pp. 24-25; Jakkrit Orrasri/Shutterstock.com, p. 25; matimix/Shutterstock.com, pp. 26-27; czarny_bez/iStock/Getty Images, p. 28; zorina_larisa/Shutterstock.com (design elements throughout).

Cover: Ronnie from Singapore/Wikimedia Commons (CC BY 2.0) (flowers); paulzhuk/Shutterstock.com (seahorse); Craitza/Shutterstock.com (carpet); Cyrustr/Shutterstock.com (grapes).